WORLD WAR 2 HISTORY

True Stories of the Wehrmacht War Crimes and Atrocities

LIKE BOOKS?

Would you like them delivered to you every week?

Do you like non-fiction books on a huge range of different topics?

We send out e-books every week so we can share our books with the world!

We have books every week on AMAZON that we send to our email list.

So if you want in, then visit the link at the end of this book to sign up and sit back and wait for new books to be sent straight to your inbox!

TABLE OF CONTENTS

Introduction

Chapter 1

History of the Wehrmacht...1

Chapter 2

Wehrmacht's Polish Campaign..9

Chapter 3

Wehrmacht in Poland – A Few Massacre Stories.....................17

Chapter 4

Wehrmacht and the Soviet Union..29

Chapter 5

Wehrmacht Reprisal Raids – Some More Massacre Stories.........34

Chapter 6

Other War Crimes of the Wehrmacht..................................44

Conclusion

INTRODUCTION

The Second World War was, no doubt, one of the worst experiences mankind has ever faced. From torture to rape to murder, crimes against innocents were innumerous – Adolf Hitler, a diminutive man with the oratorical skills of a genius took advantage of a sensitive situation in the aftermath of Germany's defeat in the First World War and amassed enough power to bring the entire European continent to its knees. In the forefront of Hitler's troops were the Wehrmacht, which had some of the most elite, most powerful and most brutal soldiers in the world.

What's alarming is that these soldiers of the Wehrmacht were worse than all the others in Hitler's entourage; where the Schutzstaffel or the SS, the Gestapo and the Nazi Party members carried out the mass genocide during the Holocaust itself, the Wehrmacht were responsible for thousands of war crimes that were carried out against innocent civilians and bystanders.

What's sad is that at the end of the Second World War, when the Nuremberg Trials took place and most of the WW2 criminals were tried and then punished, the Wehrmacht was declared as not a criminal organization. This was because of a legal technicality and loophole that left them as simply part of the German Armed Forces.

However, this does not change the fact that the Wehrmacht committed innumerous war crimes against a number of people, particularly the Jews, Romani and the Slavs – from rapes to plunders to murders, they didn't hesitate to ruin their targets completely.

Just because they were ruled as 'not a criminal organization', it doesn't mean that they weren't criminals – there are even some who would deny that these men were war criminals, but that lies on par with those who would deny the existence of the Holocaust itself, given that there is ample evidence to prove the evil-doing of the Wehrmacht soldiers...

CHAPTER 1

HISTORY OF THE WEHRMACHT

Before we jump into tales of horrors that the Wehrmacht committed, let us quickly take a peek at their history and background. Who were they? How did they come about? What was the role they were initially meant to play when the Second World War actually began?

The Wehrmacht, translated as Defense Force, was the unified armed forces of Germany. They served from the years 1935 to 1946 and consisted of the usual Army, Navy and the Air Force – the 'Heer', the 'Kreigsmarine' and the 'Luftwaffe'.

Even when they were begun, the Wehrmacht were a defiance of authority; they were the Third Reich's attempt to rearm the German Nation following the Treaty of Versailles, which was constituted at the end of the First World War, which restricted Germany's power.

However, the Nazi Party was slowly growing in strength and with Hitler at the helm, they did not hesitate to rearm their nation.

The Treaty of Versailles, as I said, put a restriction on Germany's power – it stated that they could only have an army, which had a limited number of one hundred thousand men. 100,000, as is obvious, is an extremely small number of soldiers to defend an entire country – at the time, the newly created army was called the Reichswehr, under the new Weimar Republic and it was the precursor to the Wehrmacht.

The structure and the organization of the Reichswehr was interesting, especially since it was severely limited in its functionality by the Treaty. A unified entity, it was meant to have only seven infantry divisions, accompanied by three cavalry units – the navy was also part of the Reichswehr, with just fifteen thousand men. These 15,000 were augmented by a number of boats and ships; however, no submarines were allowed to be part of the navy.

What was even worse was that a general staff were not allowed to be established. The Reichswehr's capacity for combat was also limited; weapons of the heavier and powerful kind, such as 105 mm guns, (205 mm for naval guns), armored vehicles of any kind, capital ships, aircrafts and any submarines were not allowed to be part of the Armed Forces.

Germany had no choice but to comply with these terms – they were closely monitored by the Military Inter-Allied Commission of Control, right up to the year 1927.

As is obvious, such a Treaty put many of the German soldiers off of the Armed Forces themselves; the fact that only a hundred thousand men in a year could be part of the army meant that only the absolute best soldiers could make it in. This was good, in a way, but it severely handicapped the entire German nation, which was already simmering with tension and Anti-Semitist attitudes.

So it really isn't surprising that a number of those who conducted analysis of Germany's defeat in the First World War, decided to secretly continue experiments and plan 'for better times'.

Obviously, these were the forerunners of the Wehrmacht; ironically, it was the Soviet Red Army that helped them here, not realizing that the Wehrmacht would commit such atrocities against them at a much later stage.

Under the disguised name of Truppenamt or the Troop Office, a number of men such as Heinz Guderian – all of whom would go on to become leaders of the Wehrmacht – even set up a team which would execute the functions of a general staff, although they could never claim to be such openly.

This was the time that they came up with a number of ideas they would later use during the war – they quietly built the army they would then use to take control of the whole of Europe.

Once the Nazis rose to power, Hitler went on to remove the Reichswehr and instituted the Wehrmacht officially. He wanted a modern, fully armed set of soldiers who could go on the offensive, as opposed to the entirely defense based forces that the Treaty imposed on them – he wanted to regain any territory they had lost during the First World War, dominate their neighbors and then take control of the continent.

All of this required a powerful army, which had not only thousands of soldiers, but also well-equipped fighters with enough artillery and enough firepower to take on other armies. The Reichswehr had none of this – Hitler set up the Wehrmacht to be the top and then went on to institute himself as the commander-in-chief in the year 1941.

The heart of Germany's military power was the Wehrmacht. When the Second World War began in earnest and Hitler began to march on his neighboring country, his generals made use of the Wehrmacht to an effect that is known as a Blitzkrieg.

For those unaware, Blitzkrieg, translated as Lightning War, is a type of warfare where the team that is making the attack is spearheaded by a large number of armored, motorized or mechanized infantry. They are offered given close air support with a number of other crafts that allows them to break through the opponent's lines with the short and fast attacks they make on them.

With the speed that comes with these crafts, they are able to surprise their enemies and thus, the powerful force dislocates the defenses without any hassle.

This type of warfare makes use of combined arms, which is a simple way of saying that the soldiers use an approach that integrates all types of combat arms to achieve mutually complementary results – that is, the infantry and the armor, in the urban setting, compliment and augment each other's attacks.

This is also maneuver warfare, which is a military strategy that works on the principle of making fast, short attacks to take the enemy by surprise and thereby, incapacitate their decision making process by not allowing them to recover between attacks.

Blitzkrieg is both combat and maneuver warfare, which makes it a decisive Vernichtungsschlacht or a 'Battle of Annihilation'. And with the Wehrmacht, it became a deadly tool, their new military structure and their weaponry and strength crushing their opponents. Hitler reorganized them to suit his needs – he gave them powerful armament, had them trained to be the strongest, fastest and most brutal soldiers so that they could take their opponent down quietly, efficiently and ruthlessly.

When they were at the height of their power in the year 1942 and were focusing on expanding territory and capturing more and more of the European continent for themselves, the Nazis owned almost 400,000 square kilometers of territory that they had managed to conquer.

With the SS augmenting their efforts, especially on the Eastern front of the War, the Wehrmacht forged on ahead and committed numerous war crimes – ironically, despite all evidence, they even went on to deny that these crimes had taken place.

When the war finally came to an end in the year 1945, the Wehrmacht ended up losing about eleven million men – more than half of these soldiers were killed in action, during the war. Of the leftover soldiers, only a handful of these men were actually made to stand trial for war crimes – but there is proof that more or all of them were involved in illegal crimes, despite not having been tried for it.

As the war went on, the Wehrmacht committed more atrocities. The Nazi ideology was that their race – the Aryan race – was better than every other race. Jews, homosexuals, Bolsheviks, Slavs and many, many more were all persecuted, simply on the grounds that they were born in a 'lesser' race; this meant that they propagated the idea that anyone not of their own were 'subhuman' and hence, their suffering was totally justified.

This meant that the Wehrmacht, propelled by such ideas, were not only ordered, but took joy in wiping out all these 'subhuman races'; they did not hesitate to torture, rape and brutally kill Jewish, Mongol, Asians, and any other race that they deemed not being part of their own.

The SS and the Nazi political party tend to get more attention, given that they were the oppressors when it came to rounding up the condemned innocents and then pushing them into concentration camps, where they were forced into gas chambers to be killed, if they were not made to do back breaking work which would destroy them first.

These are the factions that gain most attention when it comes to dialogue about 'The Final Solution to the Jewish Problem' – they are often tasked with responsibility for murdering millions, either through gassing or shooting innocents on sight. In the aftermath of their paramilitary death squads, most people overlook the war crimes that the Wehrmacht perpetrated against the innocent villages they conquered.

Like any army that conquers and defeats the enemy, the Wehrmacht also took to plundering and looting their new territory. This is, perhaps, understandable – but they did not simply loot and plunder. They turned into brutal, savage animals and decided to play with their victims, torturing them and destroying them completely.

This was especially true of their conquest of Poland and in their fight against the Soviet Union, both of which we shall discuss in the later chapters.

The Wehrmacht, of course, did not act in isolation – what made things worse was that they worked in cooperation with the SS itself.

Franz Halder, who was then serving as the Army's Chief of Staff General, went on declare in one of his directives that, if there were any guerilla attacks, then the German troops must impose 'collective measures of force', which was a euphemistic way of saying that they had the full permission to go ahead and massacre entire villages in retaliation.

The SS cooperated and augmented the Wehrmacht's efforts by keeping the killing squads well supplied – they gave them artillery, weaponry, ammunition, along with providing other support services such as transport and even housing at certain times.

Apart from the Jews themselves, the Nazi regime also targets other people and prime amongst these were the Communists and the Partisan fighters, who were murdered in their sleep. They were hunted down by both the SS as well as the Wehrmacht – evidence of this comes from the personal journals and diaries that many of these German soldiers kept as a log of their activities on the battlefront.

Historians claim that anywhere between 300,000 – 500,000 people were killed when the Wehrmacht launched their anti-partisan war in the Soviet Union in their attempt to gain control. Thousands of innocent Soviet civilians starved to death because the Wehrmacht soldiers requisitioned supplies, food for the soldiers themselves and fodder for their draft horses.

As you can see, they were hardly innocent, despite all the claims to the contrary. We will examine some of their war crimes in detail in the later chapters, but to complete a background study on them, I shall tell you that they were brutal, hard and enjoyed torture. Fortunately, the way drew to a close soon enough, with the Allies slowly but surely gaining ground.

The Allies, particularly the British officials, came to know that these Wehrmacht men were not innocent, when they listened in secretly on the conversations between the German soldiers and generals they had taken into custody.

They came to the sickening realization that the German Armed Forces had not only fought the war and gained territory, but had committed murder and were guilty of horrific war crimes in their campaigns throughout Europe. Many of the British and American soldiers taped conversations between these men who were taken as Prisoners of War – these tapes serves as evidence to prove that many of the Wehrmacht took part in these atrocities voluntarily, especially when it came to attending and jeering at mass executions.

Fortunately, by the time the month of September in the year 1945 rolled around, the Wehrmacht had, more or less, ceased to exist. It was an organization functioning only in name; however, it was only in the August of 1946 that it was officially dissolved.

When they unconditionally surrendered to the Allied Forces in 1945, a few of the Wehrmacht units continued to remain active. Some were independent, such as the unit functioning out of Norway, but most were placed under Allied Command as police forces for them.

After the Second World War came to a complete close, the Wehrmacht was shut down and never had a successor. When Germany reinstituted its armed forces after the war, it was split into two factions – the 'Bundeswehr' that belonged to West Germany and the 'National People's Army', which protected East Germany. Neither of the two factions took to the Wehrmacht's ideologies – they completely shunned their legacy and forged new traditions and practices of their own, which would reflect the newly instituted Germany instead of the Nazi Germany.

What's interesting is that these two factions actually employed the men who had been part of the Wehrmacht. Those who had not been tried, who were still in Germany and looking to be part of the military even after the war – they were all drafted into the new Armed Forces. However, neither organization considered themselves to be any kind of successor to the Wehrmacht; they swore off their legacy and operated on their own.

In the end, the Wehrmacht were a brutal force that crushed millions of people in their attempt to gain territory for the Nazis. Many people deny that these men took part in committing innumerous war crimes, but we cannot turn our backs to the reality – they did brutalize, victimize and hurt thousands of innocent people on the countryside as they marched on territory to conquer Europe.

CHAPTER 2

WEHRMACHT'S POLISH CAMPAIGN

Poland was one of the worst affected by the Wehrmacht and their atrocities. As we saw, the Wehrmacht were the Armed Forces of Nazi Germany, who marched in armies on the territory Hitler and his generals wanted to conquer. It goes without saying then, that, the majority of their war crimes were carried out on the battlefront, where they took on other armies and defeated them to mark their territory.

Poland was one of the very first territories that the Germans occupied. Obviously, the Wehrmacht fought the Polish soldiers and tortured millions of civilians as they rampaged through the countryside.

Murder of Innocent Civilians

The Wehrmacht killed hundreds and thousands of Polish civilians as they moved through the countryside during their September Campaign in the year 1939. If they were not executing men from the rebel factions or the Resistance, they were dropping bombs on Polish cities to terrify them into submitting to the Nazis.

If any Polish citizen, civilian or otherwise, attempted to protest or be defiant, they were dealt with quickly and brutally, with the most ruthless type of violence. This was because the Wehrmacht – and by extension, the Nazis – wanted to make an example out of any person who would stand against them. They wanted to establish their superiority without question.

Interestingly, the Army leaders are said to have discouraged their men from shooting randomly – they did not want any 'wild shootings'. This stands testament to the fact that the Wehrmacht were going out of control; they would go around, shooting innocent Poles on their own initiate, indiscriminately destroying innocent lives without any actual rhyme or reason.

However, despite the fact that their leaders ordered them to put a stop to it, this control never went any further than the order itself – some of the Wehrmacht, who were proved to have randomly shot at civilians, were put through a court martial. Don't be fooled; the proceedings were nullified against these junior officers very quickly, because Hitler himself ordered it.

He stated that any and all military personnel who had committed war crimes in Germany's trudge against Poland would be forgiven and gave them an official pardon, despite all evidence stating that they had killed thousands of innocent people.

From what we know, the Wehrmacht did not stop after the campaign itself. Even after the hostilities came to an end and Poland became an official part of Nazi Germany territory, the Wehrmacht took control of Poland's administration and went on to torture and maim innocents. They were in control till the end of October in 1939 – during this short period; they burned over five hundred towns and villages.

Close to 175 executions were carried out, and that is not even taking into account the many incidents of plunder, of looting and banditry and random shootings and murders which made no actual sense because the victims had no reason to be killed.

Overall, it was estimated that more than 16000 Poles were victims of these atrocities – of these, 60% of the crimes were committed by the Wehrmacht directly. Although their job was simply to help the SS in rounding up the Jewish population and then helping them in transporting them to concentration camps and the like, the men of the

Wehrmacht were to take matters into their own hands and massacred thousands of innocent men, women and children on a whim.

In the summer of the year 1940, Reinhard Heydrich, who was then serving as the commander of the Reich Security Office and headed the Gestapo as well, said that, in comparison to the, *"...crimes, robberies and excesses committed by the army, the SS and the police don't look all that bad."*

If the head of the Reich Security himself felt that the Wehrmacht were worse in their behavior than the SS or the police, which were systematically responsible for rounding up and then gassing millions, then you can imagine the kind of depravity these men exhibited at the warfront.

What is worse is the attitude of their superiors within the Army itself. These men were not directly involved with the war crimes being committed in Poland, but neither did they do anything to stop them, despite being well aware of what was happening. They simply looked the other way, preferring to keep their mouths shut about any of the crimes the soldiers were committing – not one of them protested on any moral grounds.

No one said that these men should be punished because it was wrong to maim innocent civilians for the sake of fun as they were doing it; if there were any protests, it came because of concerns about discipline. In fact, the general who objected the most to the crimes taking place in Poland – a man who went by the name of Johannes von Blaskowitz – did not do so because he thought it was wrong.

He protested because he felt that the Wehrmacht should not commit these crimes with the help of the SS – he was not against the atrocities, but the way in which the Army was working in tandem with the SS.

His logic was that the Army was bringing damage to the discipline of the SS – he wanted the SS to be in charge of the massacres and approved of their proceedings only, not the Army's. He demanded that the Army be kept out of the massacre in Poland and let the SS take control; the consequence of this demand seemed to be that the troops and the officers stationed in Poland took that to mean that the government was 'legitimizing' murder and massacre in Poland.

The atrocities took a turn for the worse, since both the Army and the SS began to commit these crimes, which were, technically, no longer seen as actual crimes.

Bombing of Innocent Civilians

One of the boldest and most painful acts of war that Germany carried out was the bombing of Wieluń. Wieluń is a small town in Poland – this was the first place that the German Air Force took and marked the start of Nazi Germany's campaign through the country.

The bombing of the small town is officially considered to be the start of the Second World War, particularly because the town really didn't seem to have any strategic value – there is debate on the exact strategy behind bombing the town.

Some state that there was no military target or even industrial target in the area that could give Germany a superior position in the war; there was only a small sugar factory on the outskirts of town, not to mention the fact that the Wehrmacht only bombed the hospital at the beginning, which really doesn't make sense.

However, there are others who are of the opinion that German reconnaissance soldiers had identified a Polish cavalry brigade along with an infantry division the day before the attack took place – this was what the Germans were aiming for, but due to the heavy fog, they missed these military formations and instead hit the town, which was almost destroyed completely.

Whatever the reason for the bombing, the fact of the matter is that the German Armed Forces almost completely decimated the entire place.

More than a thousand civilians were killed on the spot and hundreds more were injured – the casualty rate, whether it was collateral damage or not, was simply too high a price to pay, especially since there was no militia or strategic reasoning behind the entire attack.

Soon after, the Wehrmacht, particularly the Luftwaffe division of it, went on to bomb cities across the entire of Poland, from Warsaw to Frampol to a number of other places. Millions of innocent Polish civilians were killed; what is sad is that these air raids were not considered to be official war crimes since no customary international law with respect to aerial warfare existed during the times.

It was only after the Second World War that these kinds of laws were set up – this meant any of the soldiers who bombed cities, whether strategically or otherwise, were not persecuted for them at all.

Brutal Murders of Polish Prisoners of War

The most horrifically affected by the Wehrmacht were not the big towns and cities alone, which quickly surrendered to the German Forces. It was the people in the countryside who had no way of defying these men. They looted, plundered and took prisoners – the Prisoners of War or the POWs were hardly given special treatment...

If anything, the Wehrmacht loved to torture and kill these POWs. Polish soldiers were taken into custody after being defeated, but they were not treated according to the international standards in which the war prisoners are expected to be treated. They were instead, taken to be 'playthings' for these soldiers, who would often execute them randomly.

At Śladów, for instance, a small village in the southern region of Poland, over 250 prisoners of war were killed, either by shooting them or drowning them. In Ciepielów, around 300 were murdered, and another 300 hundred were killed in Zambrów. Prisoners of war who were of Jewish origin or had any Jewish blood in them were routinely rounded up – they were shot on the spot, without even being given a chance to prove their 'innocence'.

Another major campaign in Poland was the Battle of the Bzura – it served as the biggest battle that Germany waged during the September Campaign in 1939 and it brought them full control of the region. The prisoners who were then taken into custody in Żyrardów were tortured inhumanely – the Wehrmacht not only beat and maimed them, they also starved them.

For a full ten days, they were not given any food; needless to say, few survived the torture. If that was not enough, a number of prisoners were also burned alive.

Another instance of cruelty on the Wehrmacht's part was this – they apparently threw hand grenades into a school building. The building housed a number of the Polish prisoners of war who had been taken into custody; they were tortured and then killed mercilessly.

In the end, historians note that the Wehrmacht had killed at least three thousand prisoners of war during their entire September Campaign.

Rapes

In any war, unfortunately, as bad as the soldiers have it, the civilians and the innocents have it worse. The Wehrmacht did not hesitate to take what they felt they were entitled to; in a sexist setup such as the one in which they were operating, this meant that the women and girls fell into the category of 'things to be plundered'.

Like with any war, the female sex suffered horrifically – even when their own menfolk were out, fighting to protect their homes, the Wehrmacht marched into said homes and dragged them out, raping and then killing them.

It was particularly bad for the Jewish women, who were targeted because of both their sex as well as their origin. If they were taken as prisoners and sent to be executed, then they would be raped before the mass execution would be conducted for all the prisoners of war – sometimes, these rapes took place publicly, adding to their humiliation and agony. At other times, female captives that were shot on sight were often raped before they were killed by the German military.

Of the thousands of innocent girls and women who were taken against their will, only one rape case was actually prosecuted by a German court. What is sad is how the case turned out – three soldiers gang raped the women of a Jewish family in Busko- Zdrój.

When reported and then taken to court, the German judge did find them guilty – but not of rape. Instead, he accused them of Rassenschande. For those who do not know, this is the racial policy of the Nazi German nation, which stated that any sexual relation between Aryans and Non-Aryans (like the Jews they had raped) was defiling German blood and hence had to be prosecuted.

As you can see, even the moral judgments that were delivered were utterly skewered. No wonder then that the Wehrmacht were able to get away with committing as many atrocities as they did...

Widespread Plunder and Looting

And of course, as with any war effort, as they moved through the countryside, the Wehrmacht took to plundering homes and property. Not only did they steal items from the Polish homes for themselves, they also aided the war effort in this manner – in fact, until the November of 1939, the Wehrmacht packed up and sent close to 10,000 train wagons that were filled with stolen property, including but not limited to furniture, agricultural implements and machinery and even food.

In the end, the German Armed Forces treated the Polish countryside as their own personal playground. They did not care who they were harming, they did not care for any innocents and they most certainly did not care for the lives or the dignity of these people – they pillaged, looted and plundered like the cavemen of old and did not once stop to feel sympathy or empathy for the people they were murdering ruthlessly.

Let us take a look at some specific massacres they committed in Poland in the course of their September Campaign.

CHAPTER 3

WEHRMACHT IN POLAND – A FEW MASSACRE STORIES

As we saw in the previous chapter, when the Wehrmacht moved into Poland during the September Campaign, they ended up not only conquering territory, but also acting like depraved maniacs who pillaged, plundered and looted innocent homes and people.

They committed acts of complete atrocity, going about murdering and raping randomly at the slightest provocation – their justification was that these people were less than them, 'subhuman' and deserved to be treated in so callous a manner, and therefore, there would be no persecution for it. Sadly enough, a majority of them did escape persecution. In this chapter, we will take a look at one such horrific atrocity they committed, which nearly wiped out entire villages.

The Częstochowa Massacre

Just as Wieluń was bombed for no apparent reason, the city of *Częstochowa* was also nearly razed to the ground simply because the German Armed Forces did not care enough to look after the prisoners and territory in their care.

The *Częstochowa* Massacre took place on the 4th of September in the year 1939, during the Polish Campaign – it is also known by the name of 'Bloody Monday', since the attack happened on a Monday and hundreds of innocent people were shot and killed.

It was the mass murder of more than one thousand Polish people – they were all civilians, who had nothing to do with the war itself. In fact, reports suggest that they surrendered peacefully to the Wehrmacht, who went ahead and murdered them in any case. Of these 1000 (a ballpark number, exact statistics remain unclear), a majority of them were ethnic Jewish people, all of whom the German soldiers singled out and then killed.

A look at the background of the mass killings leaves it even more disturbing. The Polish city of *Częstochowa* did not even fight back – they gave in to Germany peacefully without defiance and surrendered themselves to Nazi control soon after the September Campaign started out.

The Polish Army units which had been stationed within the area had withdrawn quite quickly, indicating surrender to German Forces and all the able bodied men, who could fight, had also vacated the city – they went with the Polish Military, leaving behind a population that was mostly only women, children and the older people who needed to be looked after.

As you can see, the Wehrmacht would find very little resistance when they moved into the city – this, they did in the early hours of afternoon. The 10th Army's 42 Infantry Regiment was the one which made its approach; they did not even bother to load their guns, given that the town had given themselves up and there was no expectation of any kind of resistance.

But even more than that, the Wehrmacht leaders were concerned about instances of 'friendly fire' that had taken place before – the German soldiers, who were excited and trigger-happy had ended up shooting their own men and allies by mistake. This had led to a number of massacres of civilians in the area, who were then blamed for triggering the shooting, even if they had nothing to do with it in reality.

The Wehrmacht leaders wanted to prevent such instances from

happening and ordered that there would be few weapons in use, especially since the Polish Army had already withdrawn.

On that very day, nothing happened – diaries and journals from many of the soldiers who marched into Częstochowa that day indicate that those people left in the city did not instigate any kind of defiance against the German forces. Army reports that were filed later are also in concurrence with this declaration; the civilian population wanted nothing to do with the fighting and they acted peacefully, going in accordance with every whim of the German soldiers.

They did not obstruct the army in any way, even when members of the Wehrmacht insisted on marching into people's homes and business places and turning them upside down in search of weapons and any armaments. Needless to say, they did not find any of these things and came out disappointed.

It was on the next day that things took a turn for the worse. The Regimental Headquarters of the Wehrmacht at this time was placed around 20 km south of the city. They received reports that these German units in Częstochowa were attacked by Polish supporters on two different occasions.

One, they claimed, was in the courtyard of a Technical School – this was where the 42nd Regiment was stationed and they were, apparently, fired upon. The second instance was to do with the 97th Regiment – they were in charge of guarding and herding a group of prisoners. The German soldiers stated that someone shot at them from one of the houses close to where they were operating.

What is disturbing is this fact – even though the reports that came into the Headquarters of the Regiment seem to be legitimate, when individual soldiers were later asked, other testimonies from concerned individuals, all say the same thing. There was not one person who was able to give a proper description of these supposed 'attackers' in either case.

The end result was that there was a massacre in these places – civilians were shot as the Wehrmacht soldiers 'reacted' to these 'uprisings'. A search was conducted in all these 'suspicious' houses after the killings drew to an end – the Wehrmacht could not find any weapons, armaments or even a hint of these 'attackers'.

German historian Jochen Böhler, who specializes in the history of the Second World War, thinks that these shootings were most likely justified with false accounts of Polish partisans. He states that the German soldiers, who either panicked or in their excitement shot at innocent civilians – given that their leaders had forbidden them just the day previous to have even loaded guns, probably falsified reports of partisans to make sure they did not get into trouble.

These imagined or invented attackers were simply an excuse for their own rash actions – they resulted in the massacre of hundreds of innocent lives within the city. One of the Polish people later served as an eye witness to the entire event, having been taken into captivity by the German soldiers and was part of the group of prisoners they were guarding, who had been 'fired upon.'

The eye witness stated the exact opposite of what happened – apparently, the German soldiers opened fire upon the column of prisoners who were marching. They made use of their machine guns, it goes without saying that the prisoners started panicking and began to run helter-skelter.

Obviously, this meant that there was chaos and in an attempt to curb this chaos, the Wehrmacht began to shoot randomly, trying to get the prisoners back under their control – or so they would claim. The fact was, they really did not seem to care if any of the prisoners died, given that they were the ones who had instigated the entire incident in the first place.

This shooting alone took around two hundred innocent lives – about 200 Polish, mostly Jewish, prisoners ended up losing their lives because the Wehrmacht wanted to play and scare their prisoners into submission.

But the massacre did not end there – it was spread over the entire city, different parts of the town seeing different murders. Once all the wild shootings had come to an end, German soldiers decided that they were still not done with the city. With the shootings now inciting violence, they used it as a justification to round up all the civilians, particularly the ones of Jewish origin.

One of the few survivors of the massacre, a woman named Helena Szpilman, testified to the truth in front of the Jewish Historical Committee and what she had to say was chilling...

She stated that the Wehrmacht rounded up these innocent people from within their homes – which were searched for weapons – and then forced to march to the town square. Called the Magnacki Square, it was located in front of the town's cathedral. It is extremely ironic that they would choose the town cathedral of all places to commit such heinous crimes; by the end of the day, they would desecrate the entire holy air of the place.

In front of the cathedral, where only love and warmth in the form of religion and God were supposed to exist, these innocent people were made to lie down on the ground. They were forced to lie face down and the German soldiers snarled at them, saying that if any one moved even the slightest bit, they would be shot to death at that very moment.

There were several thousands of civilians – most of them were only children, elderly people and a few women, none of whom were capable of even fighting back in any capacity.

The Lieutenant Colonel in charge of the Wehrmacht units who were carrying out the entire massacre, a man named Lt. Col. Ube, gave an estimate – about ten thousand people were rounded up and made to lie down there in front of the cathedral. Incidentally, this was also the same man who had made those reports to the Regiment Headquarters of the 'Polish partisans'. The rounded up numbers that he gave were later found to match the estimates that the few survivors and eyewitnesses testified to.

The first thing that the German soldiers did was separate the men from the women. Following this, the men were searched from top to bottom, some even made to strip and were publicly humiliated. Anyone found with anything that could be used as a weapon – even something as small as a shaving razor or a pocketknife to open cans – were shot on the spot. They were not given even the chance to defend themselves.

Any remaining men were then ordered to march into the church. Terrified and shaking, they scurried to do so, but even then, they were not to be spared. Right there, in front of the sanctuary that the church was supposed to be, the German soldiers opened fire on them using their powerful machine guns and other hand-held weapons.

Another survivor, a Henoch Diamant, who was injured himself in the shooting, stated that several hundred men died on the spot from the shootings. Around 400 were wounded and seriously injured.

What's even worse is that this entire incident was captured on film by a German photographer. He took pictures right from the time that the civilians were rounded up to them being made to wait in front of the church, to the corpses that were left lying around without even the slightest respect for the dead, as though they were nothing more than animals.

On the one hand, the pictures are evidence to the brutality of the German soldiers – on the other, how heartless was the photographer who managed to capture everything but did not protest the shootings? Or was he simply terrified, since he was only one man against the entire rabble of bloodthirsty soldiers and took those pictures as a way of capturing evidence to be presented later? We can only speculate.

In any case, the photos did not see the light of day until the end of the war. It was the Americans who managed to get a hold of them – they got them from a German machine gunner when the war came to an end.

Meanwhile, the official reports of the massacre were made. Lt. Col. Ube, in his report, stated that about 3 women and 96 men had been killed as *"…punishment action for partisan activity…"*

However, when bodies were later exhumed in Częstochowa in the spring of the year 1940, more than 200 corpses were found, which included a lot more women and children than initially stated and all of them were traced back to the massacre.

As I said before, the massacres were carried out in different parts of the city. Apart from the cathedral shootings, a number of smaller shootings took place at various points within the city – one of these was a military hospital that the Red Cross was in charge of. Hundreds of innocent patients, who could not even move from their bed, the hospital staff and workers, were all killed ruthlessly, without any shred of mercy...

When finally the Centre for Documentation of Częstochowa History did a count and tallied the number of victims, at least 600 people were found to be murdered in the city. These are men and women we know for sure were killed – actual estimates put the number of people killed at more than one thousand; around 990 ethnic Poles were murdered, with over 110 Jews also killed brutally.

But the madness would not stop there – the ghetto near Czestochowa had around 40,000 Jews and victims, who were all murdered at one go much later, though this wasn't officially part of the Blood Monday Massacre.

After the war was over, much, much later in the year 1985, an investigation was carried out regarding the massacre in *Częstochowa*. All the former soldiers in the 42nd Regiment who had been involved were called in for questioning – most of them still maintained the fact that they were shot at from the houses located close to where they were stationed before the massacre began.

However, not one of them could provide a proper description of these attackers. Worse still, one of the soldiers even admitted to the fact that he did not who these attackers were – according to the reports, they were meant to be partisans, but he stated he didn't have any idea if they were "...*soldiers, partisans or civilians.*"

A few more soldiers stated that it was a general wave of panic that had broken out very quickly amongst all the men. Every soldier ran to get their weapons and shot blindly into the crowds, not caring about whom they were hitting – they were simply stumbling about in the dark and shooting wildly. A commanding officer recalled that he had been utterly disgusted with the lack of discipline amongst his men.

These former soldiers also went on to admit the fact that they conducted searches of all the houses where the suspected 'attackers' were and not one of them were found to be hiding any sort of weapons.

They also did not even have any able bodied men who could fulfil the role of 'attacker' – the houses were occupied only by women, some children and the elderly people of the town. All of them had been left behind while their menfolk had gone along with the Polish Military.

One soldier said straight out that he, "...*never saw any partisans in Częstochowa with my own eyes...*"

The investigation was further carried out to identify the root of the second massacre that took place in front of the church. One former Wehrmacht soldier, who went by the name of Fritz S., first gave a statement that after the wild shooting and blind killing of the first massacre came to an end, he and his men went around, politely asking all the civilians to come out and gather in the church.

A couple of days after that, Fritz came back and retracted his statement. He wanted to amend it to the truth – he said that they never asked the civilians to come out, but instead, they forced the women and children to run out and then made them line up, face down on the ground in front of the church. He said in his statement, "I want to emphasize that I never politely asked any civilians to leave their homes. In fact, we threw them out."

Much later, in the year 2009, the Polish Institute of National Remembrance found a huge number of graves near Stradom station. There were about two thousand corpses in these graves; whether they belonged to the massacre or these people were killed in some other way is something that is, even now, unclear. Whatever the truth, we cannot deny that the *Częstochowa* massacre took the lives of hundreds, maybe even thousands of innocent people. The Wehrmacht may deny claim to all war crimes, but the fact is these people were no threat to them – if they had been soldiers trying to defend their territory, it is understandable, but they were simply innocent civilians who were the targets of utter brutality.

Who were those first attackers who caused widespread panic, which led to such heinous shootings? Evidence likely states that it was a few, depraved cruel German men who decided to have some fun at the expense of their fellow soldiers and the civilians – who cared if a few Jews or Poles died in the following chaos?

It was this mentality that carried the Wehrmacht through the entire war, and it was this mentality that cost millions of innocent people their lives.

The Kajetanowice Massacre

Though not on as large a scale as the *Częstochowa* Massacre, the Kajetanowice Massacre was just as brutal and swift and it was even carried out by one of the same regiments that had killed so many in *Częstochowa*.

Kajetanowice is a small village in Poland, just a few kilometres from *Częstochowa* itself – after the German soldiers were done with the city and had practically razed it to the ground, they moved on to the countryside.

Just two days after the massacre at *Częstochowa*, the Kajetanowice massacre took place. For the second time, the Wehrmacht made the excuse of random shots being fired at them – historians suspect again, that this was probably a case of friendly fire gone wrong and nervous or excited soldiers began to shoot randomly into the crowds and killed innocent people.

"They blindly shot up the houses," said one of the few eye witness survivors – all the men who were still in the village were called out of their homes, just like in *Częstochowa* and then made to gather in the open field. All the men who followed this directive of the Wehrmacht were not only gathered in the field, but then shot at point blank range and then executed.

Then, the village was burnt to the ground.

When the smoke finally cleared, around 72 victims were identified as belonging to the village – this was more than one third of the village's entire population who had been executed mercilessly. That is not even taking into account the number of people who died in the fire and the smoke; infants, children, teenagers, men, women and old people alike were found dead in the rubble, with absolutely no distinction made between soldiers who could fight and the innocent civilians who had little to do with the war itself.

Much later, one of the soldiers who had been part of the massacre confessed that he knew that the villagers were not in any way involved with the war. He said that the regiment had been given orders – they were to go ahead and kill all the villagers, even the civilians.

Another soldier had apparently commented that, *"...all Poles should be murdered when they're still in the crib..."* and thus, the village was burned to ashes with no thought, no mercy or any kind of compassion.

What is the most disturbing about this entire story is the fact that this was started because of the 'losses' the German units suffered before they began to shoot blindly into the civilian homes. These losses were the killing of two dead horses – historians suspect that the friendly fire that took place was simply these horses being shot by excited German soldiers who caught them by mistake.

In fact, the official report regarding the massacre even went on to state openly that the killing and the burning of the entire village was something that had been done because they wanted to take revenge for the loss of two healthy and powerful German horses, which had been shot by 'the villagers'.

That they would compare innocent human lives to two dead horses goes to show just how depraved these men were. Was it really a case of two horses being killed that instigated it? Or was it more than that – did some cruel German soldier decide that chaos would be fun to handle and hence kick started the entire incident by shooting at the horses on purpose?

We can only speculate, but the fact remains – an entire village burned to the ground because of the Wehrmacht.

The Ciepielów Massacre

The massacre that took place in Ciepielów is definitely one of the worst documented crimes of the Wehrmacht throughout their September Campaign. It took place on the 8th of September in the year 1939, and it showcases the depravity of the entire German Armed Forces which were swift, lethal and brutal in the way they killed innocent people.

On the 8th of September, the Wehrmacht marched into the village of Dabrowa, which is located very close to Ciepielów. This place became the site of mass murder on behalf of the Wehrmacht – what happened was this; The commander of the 11th Company of the German Forces was killed by a sniper as the men were transporting the Polish prisoners of war. These prisoners had been taken into captivity following the defeat of the polish 74th Infantry Regiment of Upper Silesia – when the officer was killed, the commander of the German 29th Motorized Infantry Division ordered that the prisoners be shot to death instantly.

Without any mercy or even an attempt to find out who shot the commander, all the prisoners of war – who were about 300 in number – were instantly executed. They were all shot as partisans.

If that was not enough, soon after the Wehrmacht moved out of the area, the SS set up a ghetto in Ciepielów in the year 1941. About 600 people of Jewish origin who lived in the area were transported to the ghetto. About a year later, in the month of October in the year 1942, every single one of these innocent people were taken to the Treblinka extermination camp where they were all gassed to death.

After they were all killed mercilessly, the empty ghetto became the site of executions on behalf of both the SS and the Wehrmacht; any time they wanted to kill innocents, they gathered them up within the ghetto and had them slaughtered like lambs. Close to 500 Poles were executed here in this manner – it was not until the Allied Powers liberated the ghetto during Operation Tempest in the year 1944 that these people found any relief.

Whether Wehrmacht or the SS, the fact remains that Ciepielów has been the site of consistent murder and massacre by the Nazis through the entire Second World War.

Every year, in September, a ceremony is conducted in the area to remember and commemorate the victims – prisoners of war, innocent civilians, men, women, children… the Nazis did not care whom they were killing as long as they were not their own men and in the end, murdered ruthlessly…

CHAPTER 4

WEHRMACHT AND THE SOVIET UNION

The Soviet Union saw some of the worst war crimes that the Wehrmacht committed – they executed hundreds of prisoners of war that they took into captivity as they marched against the Red Army in an attempt to bring Russia to its knees.

This was something that was propelled forward by the thought process prevalent in German society about the time Hitler was amassing power – too many people believed that Communism in the Soviet Union was a Jewish plot.

In fact, the Bolsheviks were considered to be *"…a gang of Jews…"* and the Red Army, which was initially working in cooperation with the German Forces, were often commented to be *"Jewish sly"*. The racism was clear even before Germany began its war effort against the Soviet Union. With the establishment of the Commissar Order, things became very clear for the Wehrmacht to go ahead and then commit war crimes against these prisoners of war.

The Commissar Order

It was this Order that allowed the Wehrmacht soldiers to destroy hundreds of thousands of Russian prisoners of war without a shred of any mercy. The sad part was that the people who were taken into custody were not actual soldiers in the Red Army alone, though they were definitely included in the list. The Order allowed the Wehrmacht to take into custody any person who was considered to be a political commissar.

A political commissar, for those who do not know, is someone who is responsible for the ideological and political education and organization, who helps in the civilian control of the military.

These are those people who educate the leaders who control the military, leaders who do not take part in the military operation themselves, on account of the fact that if the military leaders took leadership, it would end up a militia dictatorship and not a civilian rule, which automatically tends to benefit more of the population.

With the Commissar Order, the German Forces could now easily liquefy any person they considered to be political commissar. The Order was instituted under Wehrmacht command on behalf of Hitler in the year 1941 and was then distributed to all the field officers. It goes without saying that the Order, once it came into being and was enforced, ended up destroying thousands of people – they were all executed on suspicion that they were political commissars.

The Order stated that the Wehrmacht were to destroy all those prisoners of war who were considered to be the driving forces behind the Bolshevik ideology. The Eastern Campaign required that these soldiers take *"…special measures, which are to be carried out free from bureaucratic and administrative influence…"* to end the Campaign.

This was basically a euphemistic way of saying that the soldiers had full permission from their higher ups to kill the prisoners of war whenever they felt like it and they would not be questioned at all, so long as they stated that they were killing only the commissars.

The Order further went on to state that up until then, the prisoners of war had been treated according to military considerations – now they would be treated as per the political ideology, which obviously meant that the Nazis wanted nothing to do with the Russian school of thought. The *'political objective…"* as the Order stated, was to *"…protect the German nation from Bolshevik inciters and forthwith take the occupied territory strictly in hand..."*

This meant that all the prisoners of war who were considered to be commissars, along with all the prisoners of war who were of Jewish origin, were to be handed over to the SS to be killed immediately.

This was further augmented by the belief that the German commanders held – they thought that if these commissars were taken to the prisoner of war camps in Germany with the others, they would stage a coup like the one that caused Germany's defeat in the First World War. Thus, they ordered that all these men be executed.

In between the short span of July to October of the year 1941, close to 600,000 prisoners of war, whom the Wehrmacht had taken into custody, were brutally tortured and then handed over to the SS to be killed.

What is to be noted here is that Germany, at the end of the First World War had not only signed the Treaty of Versailles, but also ratified the Geneva Convention, which of course, everybody knows about. The Geneva Convention governs international behavior when it comes to handling prisoners of war; as a country that had ratified the Geneva Convention, the way Germany handled its prisoners of war was illegal under international law.

It was supposed to provide humane treatment under the Convention for all the POWs it had taken into captivity.

When this was pointed out to the Wehrmacht and the leaders, they responded with the retort that Germany was not fighting so chivalrous a war that they could do that. Field Marshal Keitel wrote that they were, *"...concerned with the extermination of an ideology..."* which meant inhumane treatment of the POWs was a given.

Although, in comparison to the previous crimes we saw the Wehrmacht commit, this one does not seem as big a deal, especially since it was more the SS which carried out these killings, the fact is that prisoners of war are meant to be treated with a modicum of compassion. Even when tortured for information, they were to be treated with some dignity – the Wehrmacht, which had instituted the Order in the first place, afforded them no dignity or even respect.

They did not even bother to bury the corpses of the men they killed. Add to that the fact that many of these prisoners they took were not even real commissars; the Wehrmacht rarely conducted effective searches or found proper evidence to the truth. Instead, they took anyone who was suspected of being one and simply killed them – who knows how many innocent people lost their lives because of such callous attitudes?

What is interesting is that neither Japan nor the Soviet Union had signed the Geneva Convention – the Germans could not expect that their prisoners who were taken into captivity would be treated with the same humane treatment, as they were legally obliged to give their prisoners of war.

Interestingly, the Wehrmacht ran prisoner of war camps in the west, which strangely satisfied most of the humanitarian law that the international convention ascribed of them; it was on the Eastern front that they outright ignored the law and as such, committed international crimes as they tortured and executed the prisoners under their care.

By the time the December of the year 1941 rolled around, more than 2 million Red Army men had been taken into custody as the German POWs. These men were placed in camps that definitely did not meet international standards as the ones Germany was beholden to uphold.

The men who were held at these camps were malnourished and were falling prey to a number of deadly diseases such as typhus, particularly due to low immunity power and close quarters. Obviously, these issues stemmed from the fact that the Wehrmacht did not give them proper or even enough food, did not provide comfortable lodging that were safe or sanitary and offered no health care when they fell sick, which meant that illness spread very quickly amongst all prisoners in such cramped spaces as the ones they were kept in.

The regular torture of beatings and whippings were accompanied by public humiliation. Worse still, all the Jews, all the commissars and 'intellectuals' were killed outright by the Wehrmacht – if they did not murder them on the spot, they handed them over to the SS, who did the job for them.

The Muslim prisoners of war were also shot on the spot; while the Wehrmacht were wary of the Jews, most of the Muslim POWs were circumcised; the Nazis were worried that these men may or may not be Jewish.

They felt that it was alright for these men to be shot, rather than run the risk that an intelligent Jew might escape by pretending to be a Muslim – a circumcision hardly served as true identification and they believed that losing actual Muslims as collateral damage was preferable to Jews escaping death.

According to an RHSA report that was submitted on the 5th of December in the year 1941, the Wehrmacht had handed over close to 16,000 Soviet prisoners of war to be liquidated. By the time the war drew to a close, almost 6 million Soviet soldiers had been taken as prisoners of war, and of these at least 3 and a half million died in captivity.

The Wehrmacht were brutal in their handling of the POWs. They not only followed missives, they believed in what they were doing – with directives like the Order, they came to truly accept themselves as being better than their prisoners and even wrote home about these 'subhumans' whom they were correcting.

That humanity could become so depraved is truly frightening – they did not care for any suffering they caused, torturing, maiming and killing these people ruthlessly...

CHAPTER 5

WEHRMACHT REPRISAL RAIDS – SOME MORE MASSACRE STORIES

As the German Army, the Wehrmacht were at the forefront of stemming any uprisings. A large number of war crimes were carried out when these soldiers were dispatched to quell reprisal and defiance on the part of their captives – many of these reprisal raids went from simply quelling rebellion to outright massacre of innocent people. Here are two cases of such reprisal raids that went completely out of hand.

What's even more disturbing is the fact that many a time, these reprisals were not even true defiance tactics; sometimes, the German Forces themselves instigated the massacre by opening fire randomly on the villagers who would defend themselves. This defense was often cited as defiance instead and killings were carried out enmass.

The Kommeno Massacre

The Kommeno Massacre was one of the worst war crimes the Wehrmacht propagated. The village of Kommeno is in Greece, which was actually the site of a number of reprisal raids on behalf of the Wehrmacht. In this particular village, the 12th Company of the 98th Regiment of the Wehrmacht torched the entire place, killing hundreds of innocent villagers.

On the 12th of August in the year 1943, two men from the Wehrmacht were sent on a reconnaissance mission through the countryside. There, they came into contact with a group of *andartes*. For those who do not know – andartes were the guerrilla warfare fighters.

Greece, as a country, is one that is mountainous in nature; the number of opportunities the natural terrain provides for guerrilla warfare has made it a traditional part of their culture. Guerrilla warfare and andartes date back to the Ottoman period – these soldiers are often considered as folk heroes and held on a pedestal. Needless to say that when the war started, it was these men who were at the forefront of the entire Greek Resistance.

Whether these two Wehrmacht men actually saw guerrilla fighters or not, we cannot be sure. All we know is what they reported back to the head office that evening – the head office was located in Ioannina and in the evening, they came back to tell their commanding officer, Colonel Josef Salminger that they had seen these guerrilla fighters.

The Colonel, who was in charge of the entire 98th Regiment, gave the order that the 12th Company attack the village the very next morning. The leader of the attack was to be a man named Roser, who was a Lieutenant – at the very outset of the attack; he shot the village priest mercilessly.

Man, woman, child – the Wehrmacht made no difference as they shot all those who came in their way. Reports suggest that they killed close to 75 children who were under the age of 10.

A number of the villagers tried to escape by swimming across the Arachthos River – their lives were saved, but they lost their homes since the village was almost completely decimated by the Wehrmacht. The soldiers, in their first report after the massacre, said that around 150 civilians were killed – as the report went from one commander to another and moved up the chain of command, it kept changing, to the point that the 150 civilians soon became 150 *enemy*, even if most of them had been only civilians and innocents who had nothing to do with the war itself.

Close to 320 villagers were murdered that day – their names are recorded in the marble monument that was erected to commemorate the victims and is now put up in the village square.

Did the soldiers truly see guerrilla fighters? If they did, why did these fighters not come to the aid of the villagers who had been accused of hiding them and therefore lost everything? Or was it all just a plot by the Wehrmacht to torture, maim and kill innocents? We do not know the truth, only what has been reported.

The Vinkt Massacre

The Vinkt Massacre has been noted as one of the worst war crimes the Wehrmacht had ever perpetuated. This took place in the villages of Vinkt and Meighem, both of which are located close to one another in the country of Belgium.

These crimes happened between the 26th to the 28th of May in the year 1940, during the Battle of Lys – almost 150 civilians were taken captive and then deliberately killed by the Wehrmacht troops who were from the 337th Infantry Regiment. It was later stated that these killings were carried out as retaliation for the Resistance that the Belgian Army put up within the villages.

The Battle of Lys was taking place in earnest in the year 1940. For those who do not know much about it, the Battle of Lys was the final major fight between the Belgium and the German Forces. The Belgian troops fought hard and desperately – but they were unable to defeat the German Armed Forces and ended up surrendering on the 28th of May to Nazi Germany.

Now, as this battle was taking place, the German Forces began to advance in the western direction – they pushed back not only the Belgian Army, but also the British Expeditionary Force, which was aiding the Belgian soldiers and trying to help them escape to Dunkirk.

In this movement, the village of Vinkt became an important strategic point – not only was it located on the road that went south from Gent to Lille, it also lay astride the Schipdonk Canal. Now, the thing about the Canal was that it blocked the Germans from advancing further into the west – if they gained control of it, they would easily be able to defeat the Belgian Forces and take control of the entire territory they were fighting for.

Added to this was the fact that France had fallen by the time the 25th of March came around. The Battle for France had been lost – if the Belgian forces were fighting now at all, it was only so that they could prolong the war in an attempt to help the British Forces retreat from the onset of the Germans. Belgian morale was, it goes without saying, running very low.

Now, it was this torn down and battered army that was standing guard over the Schipdonk Canal. The regiment that was protecting it from the German Forces to try and stop them from gaining further advancement to the west was the 1st Belgian Division of the Chasseurs Ardennais.

In those days, it meant that it was this division that consisted of five regiments overall – of these five, one was filled with tanks and the rest of them were motorbike riders and cyclists. What is interesting is the fact that this particular regiment ended up being one of the most motivated in the entire army – despite the low morale that was spreading everywhere else, these men stood firm and protected the Bridge as best as they could.

It would have, perhaps, been a much better idea to destroy the entire Bridge instead of standing guard over it. As a strategic move, it made sense – such a thing would have, at the very least, slowed the German Forces down, since they would have to find some other way through the Canal and past it.

Instead of doing this, however, the Belgian command decided that they would keep the Bridge standing, not because they were stupid or unintelligent, but because they were as humanitarian as the Wehrmacht were not.

These Belgian soldiers wanted to help as many of the British stragglers as possible – given that the entire Belgian Army was now fighting only to protect the British retreat, it made sense, they reasoned, that they should stand guard and help any of the British soldiers who had been left behind as they tried to escape the German Forces to the west.

Of course, it was not just the British men they were protecting – a number of Belgian refugees were also trying to flee the area, and these soldiers stood firm in their conviction to help them get across. More than one million Belgian people had become refugees by this point and these soldiers wanted to help their fellow countrymen – who were mostly on foot, since their horses, cars and any other means of transport had been requisitioned by the armies.

 However, the massacre that was to follow made things worse; another additional one million Belgian people fled the now-Nazi occupied country, leaving the numbers to round up to around 30% of the whole of the Belgian population leaving the state.

As the Belgian soldiers stood guard over the Bridge, the German Forces arrived. On the 25th of May, it was the 225th Division, which would begin the massacre. These men of the Wehrmacht were soldiers, certainly, but they were not trained all that well. They were from the German town of Itzehoe, which is in the North of the Hamburg area, and they were not used to the terrain of the Vinkt region. They found it extremely hard to cross the Bridge, both due to the resistance as well as the natural terrain.

Their solution to the problem was chilling – they grabbed about 140 civilian people and then used them as human shields. The Chasseurs Ardennais – the Belgian soldiers who were standing guard over the

Bridge – fought back as valiantly as they could. They managed to harass the German soldiers and hit them with perfect precision, not allowing them to cross.

This was when a grenade was thrown into the group of hostages the Germans were holding as a threat to these Belgian soldiers – the grenade outright killed 27 of them and severely injured many others.

The battle continued over the course of the next few days – on the 26th of May, which was a Sunday, the German ended up taking hostages from not just Vinkt, but also Meighem. What is worse is that they nabbed these innocent people who were on their way to and back from the church on a Sunday, as well as from where they were working on their farms within the neighbourhood – clearly, none of them were actual soldiers, but simple civilians who were going about their daily routines in as normal a manner as they could.

A number of these men and women taken into custody to be hostages were shot and killed on the spot. But the most number of people died at the Meighem church – the entire church was held hostage and a grenade was tossed inside, which killed almost 30 people in one go.

The massacre did not end there – on the 27th of May, Hitler announced publicly over the German radio that he wanted Belgium's complete and unconditional surrender to happen as soon as possible.

The leader of Belgium at the time, a man named Leopold III who was king, knew he had lost. He went to his government and told them that as the Supreme Army Commander, he had the power to lay down the arms of the country – he announced that he was going to give Hitler what he wanted and surrender unconditionally to Germany, if only to prevent more suffering for the Belgian people.

As all this was happening, the Belgian soldiers at the Bridge, who had not had the chance to listen to the radio, were still valiantly defending their position from the Wehrmacht. It is entirely unclear what happened, since there were few survivors of this day, but for some reason, the 225th Division of the German Forces now not only took hostages in front of these men to force them into submission, but also went on ahead to execute them.

They grabbed innocent people and then killed them on the spot – these refugees were taken at random from the columns of people who were trekking south and then made to stand in front of the bridge where they were executed.

On the morning of the 28th, around 4 a.m., local time, the King of Belgium, Leopold III, along with his Army, capitulated to the German Forces. But the carnage at Vinkt did not stop even then – the capitulation indicated the complete and total surrender of Belgium to Germany, but still, even after it happened, nine of the hostages still in Wehrmacht custody were shot and executed.

Out of these nine victims, five were forced to not only die, but also dig their own graves before they were shot – shaking, trembling, they dug out their own final resting places under the guns before they were finally killed.

Later on, when the dust finally cleared, a victim count was made. The numbers did not match up, since many historians tend to argue between the victims who died at the bridge and those who were murdered at the church. The problem is that the grenade that was tossed into the Meighem church seemed to be Belgian artillery – who tossed it, why it happened and who was the company behind the actual attack is entirely unclear.

Was it the Germans who were trying to frame the Belgians? Or was it a last ditch attempt on the part of the Belgians soldiers who mistakenly believed that the Germans were inside? We can only speculate...

This conflict is made worse by the fact that there are a number of survivors from the church incident who claim that they saw the German officers throw the hand grenade inside the church, which caused the explosion.

Another issue was the fact that all the female victims who were inside the church were called out – this meant that the people who died inside were entirely men only, indicating that it was probably the German soldiers who were taking out people who could have been potential fighters.

This was one story that came out of the Vinkt massacre; another witness testified to something entirely different. A priest, who had been part of the civilians who were rounded up by the Germans inside the church, had managed to escape – he fell beneath two of the corpses of those who were shot to death and pretended to be dead and thus escaped in that manner. He would later state that he saw not just men, but also the corpses of women and children – including infant babies.

Now, what is interesting is this fact – when the scene was later cleaned up, there were no bodies of women or children to be found. If the priest was telling the truth, it would imply the scene was cleaned up later.

This means that the actual death toll, in this case, was definitely higher than the estimated 140 victims – was it the German forces who came back to clean up their mess? Or was the priest lying, possibly dazed and confused from the trauma he had been forced to go through?

Some Belgian historians believe that the original estimated numbers are figures of the actual executions – if the others that the priest saw were killed, then it must have happened in the crossfire, they claim, and these victims were collateral damage, not intentionally murdered, as the priest seems to suggest. In any case, whether intentional or not, the fact remains that we honestly have no idea exactly how many people were killed in between these days in May, when the Wehrmacht took random hostages to force the Belgian Army into submitting to them.

Further, as the news of the incident spread, the German forces denied that it happened. The truth was that this was brutality of a type that was terrifying and rarely encountered – the cold callousness with which they had used innocent people as human shields horrified many, both inside and outside Germany.

To paint a pretty picture of themselves, the Nazis and the press they had on their side either completely denied the story or they excused it. They said that the Belgian civilians dressed up in soldiers' attire and had to be put down; they claimed that the Belgian Resistance was getting worse and this was a Reprisal Raid, which in a way, it actually was.

The British, of course, were well aware of the whole story, but their newspapers did not press the issue. Given the fact that the whole incident took place inside Belgium, they were afraid of being misunderstood, especially in the aftermath of the 'The Rape of Belgium'.

For those who do not know – 'The Rape of Belgium' is the term that is normally used to refer to the treatment that the Belgian civilians were put through when Germany invaded and occupied the country during the First World War. Now the problem here is that, in Britain, many publicists during that time propagated these stories on their own; while statistics later proved that they were to a large extent true, Britain – at the time – was accused of spreading war propaganda.

Again, this time, they were afraid of being accused of the same war propaganda and withdrew quietly, not wanting to be held responsible for exaggerating the truth of the Vinkt massacre as they were of the previous instance.

The Vinkt Massacre drew attention, especially on the Western Front, since it was one of the few and major war crimes that the Wehrmacht committed. It was not a special unit of the German Forces, it was not the SS or even the Waffen SS who were more infamous for these kinds of incidents – it was simply a normal soldier of the army who went ahead and killed so many people ruthlessly. It is one of the most notable crimes committed by the Wehrmacht on the Western Front.

Fortunately, it did not go unpunished – given how public the massacre became, the authorities had no choice but to put these soldiers on trial. A war trial was conducted and they were all put on the stand, though how many were actually punished is something we can only guess at.

Punishment or not, the lives of those lost in the massacre remain lost – the Wehrmacht's brutality and depravity came to the fore during this incident...

CHAPTER 6

OTHER WAR CRIMES OF THE WEHRMACHT

It wasn't just on the warfront that the Wehrmacht perpetuated war crimes. They were cruel, brutal men who were fully firm in their belief that they were better than those they were conquering; this meant that they gave very little importance to the lives of these innocent people. Like with those at the concentration camps, there were a number of other atrocities that the Wehrmacht were involved in.

Human Experimentation

If you know anything about the history of the Holocaust, you know that human experimentation was something big within the German camps, especially on POWs. Not only did the Wehrmacht know about these experiments, they augmented, helped and even conducted experiments of their own. They usually provided aid when the doctors wanted to conduct experiments in the following areas –

- When it came to high altitude tests; the doctors put these prisoners in a low-pressure chamber to simulate high altitudes in order to find solutions for German pilots who had to eject. Obviously, few survived the experiments.

- When it came to drinking seawater; the victims were made to drink nothing but seawater, since the Nazis were trying to see if this could be made drinkable. The victims became so dehydrated and starved (they were given no food), other prisoners testified to them licking floors after being freshly mopped just so they could get water.

- When it came to freezing the human body; the Wehrmacht were on a quest to find out how to stop and/or treat hypothermia and conducted a number of experiments. Few survived.

- When it came to 'treating' homosexuality; the Wehrmacht doctors wanted to 'cure' it by injecting these people with hormones and then putting them into battle.

In many cases, even if the victims did manage to survive the horrific tortures that these men put them through, they were outright killed by the Wehrmacht. They wanted to observe the changes that might take place within these victims' bodies after the experiment – this was the excuse they used to justify killing these poor and innocent souls.

Biological Warfare

The Wehrmacht were some of the prime champions for the Biological Warfare cause within Hitler's entourage. They pushed the idea forward and tried their level best to influence Hitler's decision into studying it – at the time; he seemed to be considering it only as a form of defense. The Wehrmacht pushed for it to become an offensive strategy.

The head of the Science Division of the Wehrmacht was a man named Erich Schumann. He went on to urge Hitler to consider Bio Warfare as an offensive tactic. He said that they would have to attack America, *"...simultaneously with various human and animal epidemic pathogens, as well as plant pests..."*

It goes without saying that Hitler apparently gave the order for him to carry out his experiments – lab tests were prepared for the Wehrmacht soldiers to use diseases like anthrax, cholera, typhoid and even the plague. They even considered using the foot and mouth disease against the British Forces.

How much of this came to fruition is unclear, given that we don't have many reports of Germany's Bio Warfare effort. But we can be sure that many victims that these experiments were carried out on were definitely innocents transported to the concentration camps where they were treated as disposable toys for the Nazis to pick up and play with on a whim.

Wehrmacht's Brothel System

The Wehrmacht began a widespread system of forced prostitution and sexual slavery. They set up brothels where they forced the females they took into custody – these women had no choice but to serve as sexual slaves for anyone they were asked to service.

One of the main reasons for this system being set up was the chronic fear they had of STDs and masturbation – the Chief Field Doctor of the Wehrmacht also stated that the danger of 'homosexualism' was spreading and perhaps having brothels would curb that.

In fact, reports suggest that mass raids were carried out in occupied territories, where young girls were kidnapped and taken into custody, precisely with the purpose of setting them up in these brothels, which were frequented by the German soldiers and officers alike.

There was one report by the International Military Tribunal, which suggested that in the city of Smolensk, which the Germans had taken, the officers not only opened a brothel, but also dragged the women of the area into it by their arms and hair, kicking and screaming.

Perhaps the worse aspect of this entire idea is the fact that none of the Wehrmacht were actually persecuted for the sexual violence they propagated. During the Nuremberg trials, many of the soldiers were let go on the grounds that rape was defined to be a crime against humanity

– but prosecuting it did not come into play, since these crimes were not a nexus to war.

The Nuremberg Trials were war trials, and that meant that anything that was not 'war' was not persecuted, no matter how many girls lost their lives, their very self-respect and dignity in the aftermath of being forced into sexual slavery.

The Wehrmacht, as you can see, were some of the worst people in Nazi Germany – they plundered, looted, killed, tortured, maimed, raped and brutalized innocents without thought or mercy...

CONCLUSION

In the end, the Wehrmacht are often overlooked in the wake of the SS or the other factions of the Nazis who gassed millions of people to their deaths. But the fact is that the German Armed Forces, which fought the battle for Hitler on the warfront, were no less brutal or cruel than the rest of the Nazi Party – they did not hesitate to kill or plunder where they could.

The worst of it was that they truly believed in their own superiority and everything that Hitler said. Many wrote home about the 'subhuman' species that they were destroying or correcting and the horrific callousness with which they identify people who are simply different from them is spine chilling and reveals just how depraved humanity can get.

If you enjoyed this book, do you think you could leave me a review on Amazon? Just search for this title and my name on Amazon to find it. Thank you so much, it is very much appreciated!

OTHER BOOKS WRITTEN BY ME

Below you'll find some of my other popular books that are popular on Amazon and Kindle as well. You can visit my author page on Amazon to see other work done by me. (Cyrus J. Zachary).

World War 2 Women

World War 2 Women – Book 2

World War 2 Submarines

World War 2 Submarines – Book 2

Holocaust Survivor Accounts

Holocaust Survivor Accounts – Book 2

Holocaust Rescuers

Holocaust Rescuers – Book 2

Holocaust Survivors Box Set

You can simply search for these titles on the Amazon website with my name to find them.

LIBRARY BUGS BOOKS

Like books?

Would you like them delivered to you every week?

Do you like non-fiction books on a huge range of different topics?

We send out e-books every week so we can share our books with the world!

We have books every week on AMAZON that we send to our email list. If you want in, then visit the link below to sign up and sit back and wait for new books to be sent straight to your inbox!

It couldn't be simpler!

www.LibraryBugs.com

If you want books delivered straight to your inbox, then visit the link above and soon you'll be receiving a great list of e-books every week!

Enjoy :)

CYRUS J. ZACHARY

Cyrus is a very avid history buff but his biggest joy is the interesting history of our World War's. For the last 2 decades Cyrus has dedicated himself to continue learning and applying his knowledge to his books.

His books are written from an angle so as to give the reader maximum entertainment and information in the most effective format. Cyrus believes the more you learn the more you grow, so he always instils that in every book he writes.

Cyrus likes to call Ireland home where he spends his spare time hiking and enjoying the countryside with his family.

23881948R00036

Printed in Great Britain
by Amazon